T0208892

DEAD PEOPLE TALKING

The Incredible Stories of Men and Women Who Have
Survived Death or Near Death and Lived to Tell Them

DR. JOHN HAART, PHD

WESTBOW
PRESS®
A DIVISION OF THOMAS NELSON
& ZONDERVAN

WestBow Press books may be ordered through booksellers or by contacting:

WestBow Press
A Division of Thomas Nelson & Zondervan
1663 Liberty Drive
Bloomington, IN 47403
www.westbowpress.com
1 (866) 928-1240

Scripture quotations are from the Revised Standard Version of the Bible, copyright © 1946, 1952, and 1971 the Division of Christian Education of the National Council of the Churches of Christ in the United States of America. Used by permission. All rights reserved.

Interior Image Credit: John Rolando

ISBN: 978-1-9736-8516-6 (sc)
ISBN: 978-1-9736-8518-0 (hc)
ISBN: 978-1-9736-8517-3 (e)

Library of Congress Control Number: 2020902345

Print information available on the last page.

WestBow Press rev. date: 02/20/2020

Contents

Part One
After Death Experiences: Survivals

Part Two

Near Death Experiences: Survivals

Going back to the Author's Death and Survival

Reviewing the story of my survival of death as illustrated in Dead Man Watching, 2017: the episode began on a chilly afternoon on a hill in our northwestern Ontario town. We had rented our farm and moved into town to work in St. Anthony's, a Canadian and Italian parish. I was on my way home from another day of teaching at a local high school. Climbing up the steep hill with walls of snow on either side, I noticed an occasional, sharp pain in my chest, which eventually dissipated upon resting for a few minutes. After five separate stops, I made it through the front door of our home. Very strange . . . What was that all about?

I did not think too much more about it for that night; however, that all changed the next morning. (The statistical numbers on the most common time of heart attack is early morning.) I got out of bed with serious chest pains, sweating, nausea, and dry-heave vomiting. (At that time I did not know it, but these are the classic signs of a heart attack.) When I hit the floor at the top of the stairs outside my bedroom, our very concerned daughter helped me up and insisted that we should drive to the closest hospital only two blocks away.

(This is the point of serious caution about what to do next with a suspected heart attack. Never drive yourself or allow someone to take you. You need medical help immediately. CALL AN AMBULANCE . . . TO SAVE YOUR LIFE.)

Of course, being in denial that anything was really wrong, I thought it was too much trouble. (A couple of months previously, my EKG and stress test confirmed that I had no problems related to any heart or artery issues.) After all, I was only fifty years old.

The piercing chest pains continued to increase without relenting, and when we reached the doorway of the Emergency Department, I stumbled through the electric doors and fell on the floor! Staff rushed to pick me up and put me on a gurney. Hospital alert codes were broadcast in the halls, and a group of medical staff gathered around the gurney. The cardiac signals on the heart monitor in the Emergency Room were very audible, and I was soon surrounded by three nurses and an ER doctor.

Under the intensely bright surgery lights, distressed voices were shouting orders in rapid succession. Soon there were more medical staff in the small room already crowded with medical apparatus, and the orders became quicker and louder. "More oxygen." etc. (I later found that there were an increased number of people in the room because the night shift had stayed to help the day shift. Very peculiar to me at the time were the scissors which cut away all my clothes instead of just slipping them off. Obviously, time is of the essence with heart failure.)

As you can tell, by this time I was very aware of all my surroundings, and I was in serious heart attack trouble. The realization also struck me that our daughter's immediate call to my dear wife, Erin, had gotten her off a shift in a surgery unit in a nearby hospital.

At this tense moment, I saw the cardiac monitor, which visually and audibly recorded my heartbeat as it plummeted to a straight line, producing an alarming, steady whirring. It must be emphasized that this was not another sensational out-of-body experience or (after death experience) ADE. I was watching everything with my own eyes and listening with my ears from the operating table. The steady whirring sound was followed by the most terrifying sound of all! One of the ER docs said in a diminished voice, "We lost him."

(I would like to have interviewed the staff later about their impressions of all that happened that fateful day when my heart stopped, but that didn't happen.)

Erin's stealth entry must have caused the ER doctors some concern, as she was in her scrubs but not one of the official staff at that hospital. Her rather strange appearance at the time was also accentuated by her placing her hands over my heart. I was able to put my hand over hers in what I thought was a goodbye embrace as I was slipping away. As if that were not enough, during all the shouting and medical devices, the room fell totally silent as the steady beeping of the monitor was replaced by a fixed whirring sound. She was praying in tongues, glossolalia, one of the gifts of the Holy Spirit, as recorded in Scripture. "And they were all filled with the Holy Spirit and began to speak in other tongues, as the Spirit gave them utterance" (Acts 2:4).

The ministry of Jesus Christ and his apostles included praying over the sick for healing and even over the dead to be brought back to life! At this moment, Erin did not break down into weeping over the medical evidence that she was praying over her dead husband. This was the ultimate action of faith in waiting on God!

Under these circumstances, one would think that panic would be more in order for me at the thought of my death; however, all that occurred was silence, peace, and calm. To this day, twenty-five years later, I do not know how long the time was that my heart stopped, and Erin can only remember praying over me. There were no flashes of light, sounds, or sweet aromatic scents.

I woke up some time later with Erin as my first sight. I was moved to an intensive care unit with the now too familiar sound of the cardiac monitor proceeding at a reasonably steady pace with no stopping or alarms. I would remain there for five days and then be moved to a Telemetry floor with a holter monitor (a mobile EKG) strapped to my chest for monitoring the condition of my heart from another floor in the hospital.

The only comedy in this near tragic part of my story is what happened next. The small electronic device, with at least eight wires taped to various parts of my chest and strapped to my body, had a small, battery-powered red light that was slowly growing dimmer and dimmer until it finally disappeared. By the clock on the wall, it took twenty-five minutes for a nurse to rush into the room and check and see if my heart had actually stopped after it was finally noticed from another floor. I said, "It looks like I died twenty-five minutes ago, and it sure was nice of you to check on my corpse."

After a red face and convincing apology, she replaced the eight new batteries that are supposed to be dependable. All was well for awhile . . . until the same scene was repeated three more times over the course of several days. When I was finally discharged from the hospital, I did thank the staff for my good care with an honest sentiment of gratitude. When relatives, friends, and colleagues asked me about my recent heart attack, I had to confess that I "died" five times: once for real and four more times because of battery troubles.

Getting back to the true story of a dead man watching, my survival was and remains to this day a miracle! Our relative was a resident in medicine at that time, and Erin sent my hospital records to him for his consultation about what had happened. The medical record was shared with cardiologists on staff there, and their responses were significantly similar. The consensus was, "There is no way this patient survived the magnitude of this heart attack."

The medical description of my event included an anterior cardiac artery completely blocked, resulting in a myocardial infarct (MI) to 35 percent of my lower heart muscle. The Italian translation reads mortadella or "dead meat." My medical records show that the bottom of my heart is scar tissue and, according to present-day medical science, will not function again.

Thanks be to God, to this day I have not experienced the typical heart pains under stress (angina) requiring the use of nitroglycerin that could become a daily routine for heart attack survivors. I did the research in preparation for seminars to be presented to a system-wide staff of aging teachers. The resulting seminars provided some scary statistics. In 45 percent of all heart attacks, the first real sign of heart disease and/or atherosclerosis (plaque in the arteries) is DEATH! Medical science has moved far past my remote northern town experience. Today, more sophisticated methods are available to help with the diagnosis and treatment of coronary arterial diseases.

Needless to say, we remain thankful on an hourly basis for the blessing of a healthy heart life for many years. There was the statistical risk of a second episode within the same year. The actual date of this episode was the winter of 1997, and it has been twenty-three years without another heart attack.

Another blessing of this story is the fact that after many years there have repeatedly been opportunities to witness to what God has done in my life. One recent event involved a meeting with two Orthodox nuns while shopping in a grocery store. After some pleasantries, I shared some of my story, which begins with the title of this book. After listening intently to my story, they looked at each other, whispered a few words, and agreed that I should change my name! "It should be Lazarus." This scene has been repeated several times in different settings.

It has occasionally been a question in my mind as to what Lazarus would have said about his experience of death. (I'm sure that he was eager to share his remarkable story with anyone who would listen.) It is recorded that Lazarus was visited by a great multitude of Jews. After they met him, who had miraculously walked out of his tomb after being dead for four days, many began to believe in Jesus. Martha, his sister, was upset with Jesus for showing up too late and warned Jesus that Lazarus would stink with the corruption of death. "Lord, by this time there will be an odor for he has been dead four days" (John 11:39).

Introductory Texts on Death

The Meanings of Death and Survival

There are many accounts swirling around in the popular press with familiar words and phrases like died, miraculous, survivor, came to life again. Some even went to heaven and saw relatives or friends who had died before or found themselves at the brink of hell or heaven.

This book and its predecessor, Dead Man Watching, WestBow Press, 2017, are all about people of Christian faith who have actually or almost died with all the medical indicators. This description can be used in the historical sense, as with Abraham Lincoln or JFK. While there may or may not have been actual medical certificates of death, these stories are, nonetheless, about people who were actually dead or nearly dead and came to life again or survived near death. The mystery of how this happens in each case is attributed to faith and calling upon the mercy of God in the name of Jesus Christ.

"Then Mary…fell at his (Jesus) feet saying to him, 'Lord if you had been here my brother (Lazarus) would not have died.'" (John 11:32)

These testimonies are presented as reasons for hope and not as spectacular dramatizations of personal experiences. To testify in the legal sense is to provide verbal affirmation that the witness saw and/or heard specific events as he/she reports under oath to tell the truth. Under these circumstances it would be unusual for someone to falsify the details of their actual or near death experience.

It is also imperative that a clear distinction be made between death followed by survival and death followed by an afterlife experience. ADE represents After Death Experience, and NDE designates Near Neath Experience. The ADE stories have become the subject of recent movies with bright lights at the end of tunnels, sweet smells, beautiful fields of flowers and warm feelings of comfort and peace. Both the ADE and the NDE have been recorded in personal testimonies throughout history.

In modern times NDE may have resulted when a medical intervention was applied to prevent death, such as is common in cardiac surgery or the many techniques for preventing death from trauma or stroke.

These stories are recorded as well as can be stated and are true and clear accounts of the persons and actual events. Most of the names and places of their stories have been changed upon request to protect their privacy and their desire to remain without notoriety.

Following the publication of Dead Man Watching in 2017 by WestBow Press, the author was made aware by a number of providential meetings that his story was not unique. In the New Testament there are four named people who were dead for various amounts of time and were then called back to life. Lazarus is the most well known and dramatic, as his grieving sister, Martha, complained that his body would surely be corrupted and create a stench after four days in the tomb. The other three cases did not include a body that was long dead. They are the stories of Tabitha (Matt. 27:50-54), Eutychus (Acts 9:36-42), the widow's son (Luke 7:11-17) and the daughter of Jairus (Mark 5:21-43).These were all cases which brought attention to the life and earthly ministry of Jesus Christ, son of Mary and His earthly father Joseph of Nazareth.

In the personal case of the author, over twenty years ago, the audible call from my dear wife Erin was a prayer in tongues (glossiola) over my recently announced corpse. Looking back on that whole episode, the impact on the medical staff on the scene was observed to have been somewhere between shock and amazement, as Erin prayed over the patient the staff had just watched die. They had no idea who she was or how a stranger dressed in scrubs got into the emergency room without a staff ID tag. The impact was perhaps similar to some of the reactions to the raising of the dead in the New Testament accounts.

Going back to the issue of my own story of survival, which is not as rare as I originally thought, I remain eager to use the experience as a one on one evangelism tool. The standard ice breaker is "you are talking to and looking at a dead man." This is not a very common conversation starter. It is usually effective, and my audience frequently wants to know more. The first question is usually "how long were you dead?" With a smile my answer is that "dead people don't know what time it is, because time has stopped." That is always followed by "I sure am glad my next stop was not the morgue." This leads to one of my first encounters with another survivor of death story. Sitting next to a middle aged woman on an airplane ride to our winter home in Florida, the lady told me about her mother's death and her being carted off to the morgue. Her story is on page 5.

The next experience is the one that pushed me over the edge to write this book. After my typical opener, this elderly man listened patiently and asked no questions, which was not the usual response. Instead, he almost bragged that he had died on "three" separate occasions! Now I got to be the one shocked, and you will find his story in chapter one: The Death and Survival of Hans x 3.

This book is presented to the reader under the two main categories already described: ADE and NDE. The author moves forward through these dramatic stories of death defying survivals, even though there remains the following account of the afterlife of the rich man and Lazarus in the New Testament.

The Parable of the Rich Man and Lazarus

"Will they be persuaded if someone should
rise from the dead?" (Luke 16: 19-31)

"There was a rich man who dressed in purple garments and fine linen and dined sumptuously each day. And lying at his door was a poor man named Lazarus covered with sores, who would gladly have eaten his fill of the scraps that fell from the rich man's table. Dogs even used to come and lick his sores. When the poor man died, he was carried away by angels to the bosom of Abraham. The rich man also died and was buried, and from the netherworld, where he was in torment, he raised his eyes and saw Abraham far off and Lazarus at his side. And he cried out, 'Father Abraham, have pity on me. Send Lazarus to dip the tip of his finger in water and cool my tongue, for I am suffering torment in these flames.' Abraham replied, 'My child, remember that you received what was good during your lifetime while Lazarus likewise received what was bad, but now he is comforted here, whereas you are tormented. Moreover, between us and you a great chasm is established to prevent anyone from crossing who might wish to go from our side to yours or from your side to ours.' He said, 'Then I beg you, Father, send him to my father's house for I have five brothers, so that he may warn them lest they too come to this place of torment.' But Abraham replied, 'They have Moses and the prophets. Let them listen to them.' He said, 'Oh no, Father Abraham, but if someone from the dead goes to them they will repent.' Then Abraham said, 'If they will not listen to Moses and the prophets, will they be persuaded if someone should rise from the dead?"

This book is presented to the reader in complete respect of the Biblical accounts of the effect of death regarding its finality. The message is profoundly clear that "even if someone should rise from the dead" one may choose not to believe. It is the sincere hope and prayer of the author that these stories of death and near death might be of value in considering the meaning and realities of Faith leading to Life after death.

Thomas A Kempis, Meditation on Death

The Imitation of Christ

Translated by Fr. Leo Sherley- Price, Penguin Books, 1952

Book One Chapter 23, page 57

"Very soon the end of your life will be at hand; consider, therefore, the state of your soul. Today a man is here; tomorrow he is gone." (I Macc.ii, 63) "And when he is out of sight, he is soon out of mind. Oh, how dull and hard is the heart of man, which thinks only of the present, and does not provide against the future! You should order your every deed and thought, as though today were the day of your death. Had you a good conscience, death would hold no terrors for you." (Luke xii, 37) even so, it were better to avoid sin than to escape death. (Wis. iv, 16) "If you are not ready to die today, will tomorrow find you better prepared?"(Matt. xxiv, 44)"Tomorrow is uncertain; and how can you be sure of tomorrow? Of what use is a long life, if we amend so little? Alas, a long life often adds to our sins rather than to our virtue."

★This brief meditation on the subject of this book was written by a member of the Congregation of the Common Life, founded by Gerard Groote. The author was born in 1380 in Kempen in what today is Belgium. The original text was in Flemish and was first circulated in Holland. The work has been translated into many languages and is also widely known as one of the most published books since the Gutenberg Bible first appeared in Germany. There is little doubt that this text has been preached from many pulpits over the past four centuries.

How Two Family Members
Responded to Death

Bianca's Tribute to Her
Great Grandmother

A most beautiful story someone could possibly write about the death of a loved one was written as a school literature project by the author's thirteen year old granddaughter in 2019. I include it here as a touching memoir of a response to the death of her great grandmother.

Memoir, April 5, 2019

In everyone's life, there are years that they feel they will always remember because of an especially significant growth or change that they went through. Though I am young, and have not had many years to compare with, I feel that this school year especially has had many things in store for me to learn. It has been so eventful, exciting, strange, confusing and upsetting, but I know it will be one of which I will always remember, look back on, and see how it has impacted my understanding of many things, and how God was shaping me.

We moved in the spring of 2015 to take care of our elderly great grandmother, Ann, who lived with my great uncle, and were our only family members living in the city. Every Sunday after Church, we would drive to her little cozy house. We would come into the driveway, either arguing, upset, overjoyed, or just comfortable. Whatever our family had to worry about only lasted until we entered through her squeaky front door, for as soon as we walked in, we were carefree of the troubles outside the walls of her house. "We're here!" my mom would say in a tone not quite yelling, not quite soft - the perfect tone for my grandma to hear. Passing through the lifeless kitchen, we would collect the treats waiting in a jar on the counter, and then sneak into the den. All the toys that we had grown up with when we visited her, and played with tirelessly, were still there in the corner as they had always been; nothing ever changed. It was quiet besides the low volume of the television, and the slow, tranquil movements of my grandma. She would not know that we were there until we all greeted her with hugs and kisses. "Hi Grandma!" we exclaimed as we excitedly shuffled to a spot that she could see us. "Oh, hi!" she would say as a smile lit up her big blue eyes and her frail face. We hugged and kissed her. As we found our spots on the couch to watch TV with her, she would ask us questions about how we were, or comment on the TV show we were watching. When my mom made it to the den, she would greet Grandma the same way we did, and then help her to the kitchen to eat. There they would chat and my grandmother would tell her stories of all her extravagant travels, and we would often hear my grandmother laugh hysterically, reflecting on her wonderful life. She was so wise and such a sweet lady. I remember her as an old-fashioned doll, or a photo album of the best events in history. In her old age, she was such a bright light to everyone, even when she would just sit in a chair smiling up at everyone, with both her hands rested on the top of her cane. I am so thankful for this time, however, I wish that I had used this opportunity to ask her more questions about life situations, because I know that she would have been flattered, and I would have found her advice very helpful.

It was after one of the school soccer games that we went to visit her. We stepped up to the door, rang the doorbell, and after a while, she answered. She had tears in her eyes, spoke in a low voice, and was trembling. My mom and I were immediately struck with sadness as this was the most miserable we'd had ever seen Grandma. We came in and she informed us that her doctor had visited her and told her that her time to go was soon. We doubted her, but she seemed hopeless, and convinced us that, after 97 years of life, she was ready. The next month or so was a blur of soccer games, school, homework, and visiting Grandma as often as we could. She was now limited to the chair in her room, and her bed. We now would find her sitting comfortably in her rocker with her head laid back and the lamp softly shining on her. She wore a smile and her eyes were closed. It was like she was talking to God face to face and it warmed my heart to see her so happy.

One day, I remember I sat with her for a while, while she was awake. She asked me how school was and I told her about my joys with my friends. After I had told her all of the fun times in the school year so far, she paused and slowly told me to keep my friends close because they were good ones and how she remembered her high school friends. Sitting there, I began to think about how far she had come, how many people she had met and affected, and it comforted and helped me to see life with new and more hopeful eyes.

Another month and my grandma slowly became wearier and stayed stationary in her bed. She was no longer able to speak. Our other relatives came to help take care of her.

I slowly and lightly snuck into her room one day to see her sleeping as usual. I felt a calling to sit and pray with her, and that is what I did. By her side, and holding her soft, elderly hands, I prayed, thanking God for this precious woman's life, love, and light. It was so quiet in the familiar air of her room, and I felt that for the hour that I was there, it was not just me and her. God was there with us, by her side, smiling down at her like I was.

Another month and we visited quietly time and time again, watching and praying for her. Her breathing became more and more labored and I knew that it was almost time for her to meet God. She looked like she was in more and more pain with every breath.

It was now the fall break and we were ready for balloon fiesta. We went to bed early in anticipation for the mass ascension the next morning. I was awoken very early, but it was not for the reason I expected. I looked up at my mom who had tears in her eyes, and tears immediately filled mine. "She is finally released," I thought. My mom and I hugged, and before I knew it, we were all at Grandma's house. The lights were dim and the house was still. It was silent besides quiet weeping and soft and sad voices on the phone. I was not sure that I wanted to see her without life in her eyes, but I had seen her in so much pain, that I decided to see her one last time along with my siblings. There she was, so frail, and lifeless, and still. Tears filled my eyes even more as each of us laid our hand on her - first Zach, then Joel, then

Angelica, and last, me. I struggled to lift my hand, but I finally laid it on her shoulder, and the most amazing thing happened. I felt a rush of pure joy come through my hand and fill my entire body. A smile stretched uncontrollably across my crying face. I was no longer sad, because the happiness of heaven touched me for a split second. In that moment, I knew she was with God and felt more love and joy than she ever felt while she was living. I contemplated about life and death. I realized that life is such an amazing gift, but it does not compare to seeing the face of God. She lived her life well and inspired me with hope and taught me to love. She would always say that when we would visit her, that we made her day, but it was really she who made our day. It is a beautiful thing to share your life or just a fraction of it, with someone else, to help them, while also being extremely affected by that person. We have such an amazing gift from God; his love and mercy. But not only that, he has given us the ability to love for his glory.

My hand slowly slid off her shoulder as I kissed her on the forehead, and slowly left with tears in my eyes, a smile on my face, and the love of God in my heart.

Mckenzie's Message to Her Grandmother

Just before her death the following selected Scriptures were sent to her grandmother and hand delivered.

"Behold! I tell you a mystery. We shall not all sleep, but we shall all be changed, in a moment, in the twinkling of an eye, at the last trumpet. For the trumpet I have fought the good fight, I have finished the race, I have kept the faith. Henceforth there is laid up for me the crown of righteousness, which the Lord, the righteous judge, will award to me on that Day, and not only to me but also to all who have loved his appearing." (2 Timothy 4:7-8)

"For I am sure that neither death nor life, nor angels nor rulers, nor things present nor things to come, nor powers, nor height nor depth, nor anything else in all creation, will be able to separate us from the love of God in Christ Jesus our Lord." (Romans 8:38-39)

"The trumpet will sound, and the dead will be raised imperishable, and we shall be changed. For this perishable body must put on the imperishable, and this mortal body must put on immortality. When the perishable puts on the imperishable, and the mortal puts on immortality, then shall come to pass the saying that is written: "Death is swallowed up in victory." "O death, where is your victory? O death, where is your sting?" (John 11:25-26)

Jesus said to her, "I am the Resurrection and the Life. Whoever believes in me, though he die, yet shall he live, and everyone who lives and believes in me shall never die. Do you believe this?"

(1Corinthians 2:9) (There was always an affirmative "yes" to this question, when it was presented to the grandmother.)

What no eye has seen, nor ear heard, nor the heart of man imagined, what God has prepared for those who love him. (Revelation 14:13)

And I heard a voice from heaven saying, "Write this: Blessed are the dead who die in the Lord from now on." "Blessed indeed," says the Spirit, "that they may rest from their labors, for their deeds follow them!" (Romans 14:7-9)

"For none of us lives to himself, and none of us dies to himself. For if we live, we live to the Lord, and if we die, we die to the Lord. So then, whether we live or whether we die, we are the Lord's. For to this end Christ died and lived again, that he might be Lord both of the dead and of the living." (Philippians 1:21-23)

"For to me to live is Christ, and to die is gain. If I am to live in the flesh, that means fruitful labor for me. Yet which I shall choose I cannot tell. I am hard pressed between the two. My desire is to depart and be with Christ, for that is far better." (Revelation 21:4)

"He will wipe away every tear from their eyes, and death shall be no more, neither shall there be mourning, nor crying, nor pain anymore, for the former things have passed away." (James 1:12)

"Blessed is the man who remains steadfast under trial, for when he has stood the test he will receive the crown of life, which God has promised to those who love him." (Psalm 1:1)

"So is it with the resurrection of the dead. What is sown is perishable; what is raised is imperishable. It is sown in dishonor; it is raised in glory. It is sown in weakness; it is raised in power.

It is sown a natural body; it is raised a spiritual body. If there is a natural body, there is also a spiritual body." (1 Corinthians 15:42-44)

"You have been born again, not of perishable seed but of imperishable, through the living and abiding word of God; for all flesh is like grass and all its glory like the flower of grass. The grass withers, and the flower falls, but the word of the Lord remains forever." (1 Peter 1:23-25)

And he said, "Naked I came from my mother's womb, and naked shall I return. The LORD gave, and the LORD has taken away; blessed be the name of the LORD." (Job 1:21)

PART ONE

After Death Experiences:
Survivals

CHAPTER ONE

The Death and Survival x 3 of Hans

After sharing my story and talking about the recently published book, Hans just listened carefully but said nothing in response to my incredible story. Then without hesitation he said "Good for you, but you know I died and came to life again on three separate occasions." That statement sure got my attention, while visiting at the coffee and doughnuts social after Mass.

Hans started his personal witness of how faith in Jesus Christ as his Savior and Lord was the central focus of his life. He then moved on with the story of his first trip to an ER. He had died. The medical staff in the ER transported him immediately to Neurosurgery for what sounds like a scene from a modern horror movie. The top of his scalp and skull were removed to release the tremendous pressure of the rare double stroke, which had caused his death. After a period of resuscitation and stabilization his skull was replaced and scalp was sewed back in place. There was no question that he was telling the truth as the visible evidence of the procedure was quite apparent from the almost hidden scar on his forehead. Human beings often die from a stroke affecting one side or the other, but this survival was truly remarkable. There was only the slightest indication of residual damage, as his speech--like my own--was slightly hesitant at certain points in his story.

His second story was less dramatic but equally incredible. His body was dragged lifeless from the bottom of a swimming pool. A quick check for a pulse and respiration provided no evidence of life. The lifeguard on duty went ahead with artificial respiration as best he could. After prolonged efforts without response the lifeguard had almost given up, when a large amount of water was forcibly discharged, and Hans began to breathe on his own again.

The third and perhaps most spectacular survival was an extremely painful episode with evidence that remained clearly visible. Severe burn victims have telltale damaged skin: the surface is mottled and looks like the outside of a prune. The top of his shirt was slightly opened to expose the evidence of the extremely painful burns that covered the greater part of his body.

Hans had worked for years doing flooring of all kinds. On the fatal day of his last job he was trying to remove some very stubborn carpet from a cement floor. The flammable solvent he was using to peel up the rug reached a space heater nearby, which caught fire and engulfed the room in flames. He was pronounced dead by suffocation at the scene of the accident, but an observant ER staff member detected minute signs of life. Hans spent an entire year and a half in rehabilitation. The initial painful survival took weeks of careful treatment. Months went into extended periods of skin graft surgery with limited undamaged areas to replace the painful and scorched skin. I was practically in tears by the time he reached the end of his story and I could see that it was not easy to move through the memory of the trauma. He ended on the note that God had spared his life these three times and he could only thank Him with the rest of his life and prayer.

CHAPTER TWO

The Death and Survival of Betty

While chatting about winter stays in Florida over many years to the lady next to me on a flight, I was able to slip in my typical opener about my death at age fifty, when the topic moved to retirement and old age. After listening carefully to my testimony, she looked over to me and with tears in her eyes told me about the death of her dear mother in Florida.

She had boarded an ambulance with her eighty year old mom. All the medical indicators were standard for a massive heart attack and impending threat to her life. The ambulance crew did all the typical protocol in transit, and by the time Betty was rushed into ER, it was clear that the end was near. However, the lady telling me this incredible story was a self-professed Catholic and from a family of prayer for several generations. With modern telecommunications the whole family was alerted to pray for mom, grandma and great grandma. The waiting room scene included a few other family members from nearby.

There were no conversations expressing anxiety and "what

if" reactions. The family members continued to pray the rosary. The fateful appearance of one of the ER doctors included the results of all of their efforts to save Betty's life with care and concern. The heart attack was fatal and she died without pain and prolonged suffering.

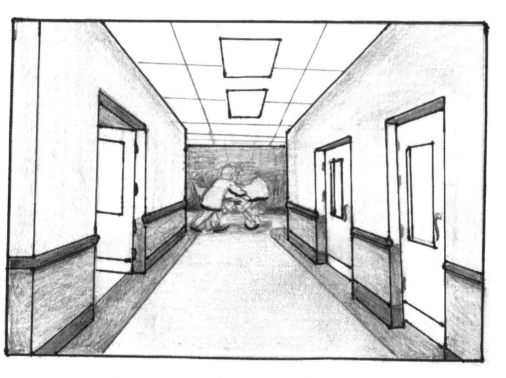

Doctor wheels the corpse to the morgue

The family was surprisingly unshaken by this news and could only share the joy that mom had gone to be with the Lord. However, after awhile the silence of the waiting room was shattered by a doctor from the morgue who came out shouting. "She is still alive. I can hardly believe it!"

Doctor walking towards waiting room

There had not been time for a death certificate to be filed, but the time of death was recorded as 10:02 a.m. The family noted that the time on the waiting room clock when the doctor from the morgue had burst in with the news was 10:17 a.m. So, Betty had been clinically dead for fifteen minutes. Follow up examination of Betty's survival showed no impairment or lack of mental functions or abilities.

This flight was different from the many other returns to our summer place. I am happy to report this conversation as another incredible story of the impact of prayer and the mercy of God's intervention in what by all definitions is impossible. The Biblical description of the life and death of Lazarus relates to Betty's story of the power of prayer twenty centuries later. No medical intervention could be used to explain what had happened, but she is still alive.

The episode from the New Testament that best applies to Betty's survival appears in Acts 20:7-10.

On the first day of the week (Sunday, in Troas) when we were gathered together to break bread, Paul talked with them intending to depart on the morrow, and he prolonged his speech until midnight. There were many lights in the upper chamber where we were gathered. And a young man named Eutychus was sitting in the window. He sank into a deep sleep as Paul talked still longer; and being overcome by sleep, he fell down from the third story and was taken up dead. But Paul went down and bent over him, and embraced him said, "Do not be alarmed, for his life is in him."

Paul's immediate response was that faith in Jesus would

provide for Eutychus to come alive after he was claimed to be dead. And in like manner it can be said that Betty's daughters and others, who were praying in faith, had the same result for her.

Years of Christian ministry comedy material have developed on the Eutychus text. Any priest or pastor who is told his homily was very much like the one that Paul gave in Acts 20, or that the congregation was paying attention just like Eutychus would be forced to review the meaning of possible consequences.

Betty had been pronounced dead, and the typical concern is the amount of brain damage after an extended period of no respirations. The next question was a real leap of faith. I timidly asked how her mom came out of this trauma.

I was prepared for the worst concerning the question about Betty's status and the frequently serious debilitation of life in a wheel chair or a permanent paralysis common to stroke victims. To my great relief and joy she asked if I wanted to meet her mom and said, "She's right next to me." All this time Betty had been listening from the next seat. She gave me a coy smile and clearly demonstrated that, "I'm just fine for an 82 year old woman who once was dead but now is alive as ever." So I remain very blessed to have the privilege to recount this miraculous story of survival for all the readers of this book.

CHAPTER THREE

The Tragic Death and Survival of Michael

When a crime is the reason for a death it can only be called a tragedy. In the case of Michael's death, the crime was a brutal attack on a downtown street of large Canadian city. We first became aware of what had happened when his mother, a faithful member of our parish prayer group, called us from the hospital to ask if we could come to pray over Michael. He and his mother had been members of our small prayer group for several years. His insights and sharing were always a blessing to all of us. The news of his precarious condition was heavy on all of our hearts.

Our dear friends and leaders of the prayer group (Joseph and Clare) picked us up for the stressful car ride to the hospital hidden in the middle of skyscrapers. The location was complicated and the hospital was not the typical driveway up to a large building with "Hospital" and a large H on the roof. In this case, the real trouble was finding the front door. At street level with no obvious signs we only had our GPS to guide us to the small lobby with multiple elevator doors. We got to the sixth floor to meet Sophie for the very emotional and stressful encounter with her and then with her son Michael.

He was attending a post-secondary school not far from the hospital. He was innocently walking back to his little apartment when a group of four men walked up and began to attack him. He was left for dead after the use of multiple baseball bat strikes to his head. The tragic result was not only a crushed skull but a mutilated left hemisphere.

The terrible results of this senseless attack were similar to gunshot wound to the head on one side. The tissue damage can only be described as irreparable. The real tragedy of this crime was the police report that the one man, who was captured at the scene with the help of a passerby, confessed, "That guy we beat up is not the one we were after." It was a case of mistaken identity!

When we reached the sixth floor the scene was particularly frightening for me. All the reminders of the smells, sights, and noises of an ER ward were all too clear in my personal memory of the scene of my own death, as reported in Dead Man Watching. We were not in an ordinary ER but a brain trauma ward, specializing in stroke and head accident cases. The specialist had recently informed Sophie that she should be prepared for the worst, and that if Michael survived he would be in a vegetative state for the remainder of his life.

Upon entering his room the sight was frightening to the point of wanting to run away because of everything I saw, smelled and heard. If the ER sights and sounds of my own death were scary, then this particular brain trauma room was a horror film of flashing lights, wires and tubes inserted into a motionless body. The sight of Michael was almost more than I could handle. It took all the courage I had to join in the prayers over what seemed to be a corpse in a hospital gown. His face was distorted with eyes closed and a large cloth helmet with hoses and wires attached to blinking and beeping machines surrounding the bed. There was hardly room for the four of us around his bed. Clare took the lead in praying for God's mercy and the sparing of his life. As we continued to pray over Michael the only area to place my own hand onto his was his left hand. His hand was ice cold, and my heart fainted as I was sure he was dead.

At the conclusion of this mission of mercy there was no visible evidence that any change had taken place. We sang softly a few songs of praise and thanksgiving and left the room, as a nurse looked at us curiously, as though we were acting that a miracle would happen.

A short meeting with Sophie in the ward waiting room allowed us to pray with her in this hour of prolonged suffering. We wandered out of the maze of the hospital and drove back home with minimal conversation.

It would be the end of the week before Sophie could call with signs of hope, as his condition did not worsen but had shown some small indicators of improvement. In view of the specialist's warnings to expect death or life in a coma, this was good news.

Michael spent the next six weeks of intensive care with growing hope of return to some of his former abilities. It started with getting out of bed by himself and physiotherapy to use his right leg and hand again. With additional time and effort, Michael is doing very well for a man with only half a brain and the crippling results of this tragic crime that ends on a very positive note. Michael is making a remarkable recovery, as he is walking, talking and processing complex information. We all remain thankful for all that Jesus has done and continues to do in this precious life.

CHAPTER FOUR

The Death and Survival of Loreto

L oreto was born and raised a Catholic in a small hamlet in Puglia, Italy, the area famous as the origin of the "best spaghetti in all of Italy" because of the quality of the durum wheat (granadura in Italian) grown there. His story was brought to us by Deacon Carlo in our Canadian parish when he found out about my new book.

At a very young age Loreto contracted scarlet fever and was found dead in his bed. He was given the Last Rites by the parish priest who was present at his death. The regional, itinerate doctor pronounced him dead and signed his death certificate at the provincial magistrate's office.

The total amount of time before his miraculous awakening was not known, but he had been dead for many hours and possibly as much as an entire day. The local population in the region quickly became aware of this extraordinary event and people began to arrive at his modest home. He and his family tried without success to avoid people as much as they could.

When he began to speak words of caution to some individuals about hidden personal secrets and their errant way of life, he began to experience even more trouble than could have been expected. He was criticized in public and the parish priest had to make pronouncements at Mass about not judging what God had done in Loreto's life and why people might benefit from his prophetic messages.

There were a number of occasions throughout his troubled life in which he could not have known what he was talking about, because he was never there. On one occasion he brought a message from a man that had been dead for many years to his widow. It was about the funeral when her husband was buried in another man's shirt. It seems somewhat peculiar that this supernatural transmission should be made over an incorrect burial outfit, but it remains an event that was true and had great meaning to the widow, because she had grieved for all of those years about her husband's final judgment and where he was. Her consolation from Loreto was that the dead man was in fact in heaven and she could finally be at peace.

Loreto did not live into old age but died naturally at fifty two. His life and two deaths remain a mystery, as challenging as the many times when people in the Bible were brought to life after they were clearly dead.

CHAPTER FIVE

The Death and Survival of Jared

Jared was in a terrible auto accident and was pronounced dead in an ER of those injuries. His miraculous recovery would eventually leave him paralyzed for the remainder of his life. He testified to members of family that he saw Jesus when he went to heaven. He was told by medical staff that his life would move forward, but not as it had been. After a period in a coma he woke up to find that he had no sensations below his neck. With some rehabilitation help and a lot of help and prayer from his friends and family he was able to progress to the stage of competing in handicapped games. In fact, he managed to win medals three times in the Special Olympics.

It was surprising to find out that he is married and has four healthy children. I don't mean to sound disrespectful, and I'm guessing you are wondering also, but "how does that work when you are almost completely paralyzed?" He has become a motivational speaker and travels widely to give his testimony. There is also the amazing story of the man born with no arms or legs who is a father and motivational speaker, too. Both of these men have stories of how faith has brought them through it all.

When I found out about Jared from his uncle, he was reported to be almost forty years old and quite successful in his careers as a popular speaker and a full time husband and dad.

Actually, I found out about Jared after introducing myself as the author of a book with that title and the fact that another book was being completed with stories like my own. While I did not get permission from Jared himself, his uncle said it would be an honor to hear that this witness would become a chapter in my next book.

PART TWO

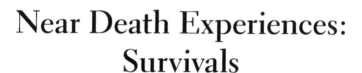

Near Death Experiences: Survivals

CHAPTER ONE

The Near Death of Jenny

This story was brought to my attention at a pro-life support dinner held near our winter home. Our life saving ministry on a street in that city happens twice a week in front of a "women's health center" (i.e., abortion clinic).

A conversation with the guest to one side was providential to the writing of this book. After hearing about my death and the book that was composed years later, Barbara started to tell me about a miracle that took place in her marriage.

In 1967 their first child was born with unusual challenges. Jenny was physically handicapped. Her body was diminutive and deformed, indicating that she would grow up as a "dwarf" with some of the typical difficulties. This condition included enlarged joints with small arms and legs. It was not discovered by a doctor at the time of birth, but she was also born totally deaf. This challenging fact was observed by a carpenter. While working on Barbara's kitchen, he noticed that the newborn baby did not respond to his loud hammering on the cupboards. Sure enough, Jenny would live all of her life without sound.

Her condition would become formidable to overcome, as well known from the Helen Keller. For Jenny the road ahead included good sight but difficulty in speaking because of a physical malformation of her pallet.

The real witness of Christian faith in this story was at the time of delivery. The doctor could have used any of dozens of considerate statements to alert Barbara of the condition of her new daughter. He said, "This child is not worth keeping because she has so many problems." May God forgive that doctor for what has now become far too common in contemporary obstetrics around the world. As a result of modern imaging and pre-birth testing many doctors suggest abortion to avoid the difficulties of a "problem child."

Barbara reacted with love, kindness and a lot of prayer and faith for her new, little, struggling baby daughter. Regardless of the doctor's apparent condemnation of this newborn gift from God, Barbara and her supportive husband would raise their new daughter in a family of love and caring.

Her witness story concluded with Barbara's smile about the recent celebration of Jenny's fifty-second birthday in 2019.

I took a bold step to ask if she had gotten married, and the answer was a surprise as big as the story: "Yes, she is married and has two very healthy children." It is essential to say that faith in Jesus Christ was and is the central aspect of this heartwarming testimony.

CHAPTER TWO

The Near Death of Daniel

At fifty years old Daniel was a healthy, athletic man with a life full of energy and risk taking adventures. This all nearly ended with a gust of wind.

He was soaring and gliding through the dazzling, panoramic skies of the American southwest desert. His hobby at that time is called backpack parachute gliding. The equipment includes a small gasoline engine, attached to a fan within a cage, which looks like a large old fashion, desk fan. The backpack weighs fifty pounds. The pilot runs along the ground until the large canopy of thin fabric fills with air and lifts off the ground.

The thrill of it all ended at fifty feet, when he was about to land, and the chute hit a down draft--common to the flight sequence. However, when this happens at a higher altitude, the chute refills with air again and works as expected. He was too low! Within seconds the aeronautic capacity to keep his two-hundred and forty pound body and the apparatus in the air became a colorful flag plunging to the desert floor below.

Even though he had been flying several thousand feet up, the descending conclusion did not leave room for the canopy to fill with the necessary air to provide for the typical soft, running landing.

backpack parachute gliding

Daniel hit the hard sand with both feet from a height that was estimated as fifty feet. The surface was as hard as concrete and the impact was shattering. Some observers called 911. An ambulance arrived twenty minutes later with paramedics gently loading him onto a stretcher. The lower half of his body was described as a "dangling pair of pants." His vital signs were good, but there was serious damage to his lower body. The excruciating pain was deadened by the body's natural protector as he went into shock followed by the use of morphine. The first ER doctor to see Daniel was amazed that he had even survived the impact.

Bone crushing landing

The damage to his lower body was substantial: two broken legs in multiple places, a broken pelvis and both ankles shattered. No wonder the first orthopedic surgeon to see him said he could save him a lot of pain and suffering by amputating both of his legs just below his pelvic area. The reconstruction program was possible but long and painful with the subscript of an enormous cost. Without insurance it would surely be financial ruin for a life time. Daniel's immediate answer was to save both legs and endure all the unforeseen problems.

The intense surgeries took many hours to complete and each one was only the pathway to the next one...months later. The installation of multiple screws, plates and stainless-steel rods took hours of surgery with several months between each recovery. Complications set in with deep bone infections requiring antibiotics in heavy dosage, resulting in the typical GI disaster. All of these problems complicated the recovery from each surgery.

Needless to say, the bill for all this specialist activity was astronomical. At the end of it all, his medical bill was one million and five hundred thousand dollars. What a blessing that it was totally covered by his insurance policy.

The answer to the many prayers for Daniel had been granted. He is now able to walk without crutches. His long recovery period had included a Christian counselor with prayer for healing.

After it all, he and several other prayer group partners took on a ministry of going to local penitentiaries to witness about the power of God in all their lives. The team is made up of men who were either wounded military or accident victims with various incredible stories of recovery.

The typical question of many about why a life is spared from death remains a mystery. Lazarus seems at first to have disappeared after his miraculous survival, but many came to him to hear about his life, death and being raised by Jesus, which became the source of many conversions.

This story leads to the next one about the pastor who helped Daniel through the mental, emotional and spiritual trauma of his fall from the sky.

CHAPTER THREE

Pastor Mathew's Near Death

Pastor Mathew's prayer and inspiration for and with Daniel was pivotal to his recovery, when discouragement was a major daily problem. The deep bone infections were long processes and very wearing.

Twenty years earlier Mathew was the youth pastor at the time of the momentous change in his life. A school bus from the small church, where Mathew served, was pulling out of the church parking lot for a picnic, when everyone inside felt a thump in the rear of the bus. Mathew was trying to help with the backup around a difficult corner, but the driver could not see him in any of the mirrors. Everyone in the bus rushed out the door at the screams of pain from under the bus. Two of the double wheels had crushed one arm, both legs and also caused a neck injury. An ambulance was on scene within a reasonable time. The paramedics quickly injected Mathew with a pain killer and carefully placed him onto a stretcher.

school bus back over

The whole church community was alerted to pray for him, and all did. He spent several weeks in painful physical rehabilitation with surprising results. The amount of daily prayer for Mathew was a major part of his rapid recovery. He continues to witness to the mercy of God whenever possible. Just to see him walking around without any impairment is a visible sign to all who know his background story.

CHAPTER FOUR

Denny's Life and Death

The Denny in this story is the same good friend that was a major part of my story in Dead Man Watching. He is the same faithful man along with his dear wife Teresa Rose, who introduced us to life saving on Tuesdays and Thursdays in Florida.

Denny was raised in a Catholic environment with no regressions or diversions. The first great challenge in his life was a diagnosis of inflammatory bowel disease at age eighteen that left him bed ridden for months. He saw life passing him by with the question of how long he would have to live with this painful and distracting condition. Discouragement was a major part of this period as anyone suffering with the condition. The medical and surgical conclusion took place at age twenty-six with a colostomy. This resection of the bowel meant that he would carry around a collection bag for the rest of his life. It was a mystery to me how he could go swimming in later life in Florida? I never quite made it to ask him this sensitive question.

He became a very successful salesman for a national brand of apparel. He married and had a family with more or less normal progress through the stages of family life. After all the time in a Catholic faith context, he had a Pauline experience at age fifty when he was inspired to quit his job and "go to work with the poor." His boss refused to accept his resignation multiple times, but was forced to hire a new man when it was clear that Denny would not be coming back.

Working with the poor was a dramatic change from their middle-class suburban life, as they traveled into Indianapolis to serve in a downtown soup kitchen operated by a Catholic organization. The clientele was predominantly requiring basic survival assistance. Daily challenges dealing with the homeless and generational poverty required perseverance, kindness, and prayer to navigate through the bad body odors, smell of alcohol, dirty faces, and drooling mouths. Then there were people in drug induced confusion.

Denny and Teresa Rose were completely out of their social element, but their selfless motivation was evident; thus, some of the people instinctively appreciated their authentic kindness and desire to help. Denny always wore a Benedictine crucifix and was approachable, and there were many requests to pray for those in need with ailments and sicknesses. A few returned each week, expressing thanks for answered prayers.

During this time the abortion disaster taking place, as a result of the pivotal Roe vs Wade Supreme Court decision to legalize the death of the innocent unborn babies, motivated the couple to become active members of sidewalk counseling. It must be emphasized that they were not protesters or picketers common to the period of protesting the war in Vietnam. Their activities were focused on offering helpful information and hope to women, asking them to reconsider their often uninformed, hasty and pressured decisions. They provided options for many practical supports, such as counseling, housing, diapers, etc. for those in need of assistance. Most of all they encouraged them to become mothers who would protect and care for their babies and, in some cases, choose adoption as a loving alternative.

All the time their ministry at the soup kitchen and lifesaving was in progress, Denny's own life was at risk due to another medical threat. This time it was multiple myeloma, a typically fatal form of cancer. He went through the only form of treatment available at the time with a lot of prayer from family, friends, and faith communities. Many years passed, when the same threat returned after an initial medical recovery from the first bout. This time he went to a Christian healing service where he was slain in the Spirit. There are many cases in the Bible of persons who were knocked off their feet and went through some dramatic conversion or change in their lives (e.g., Paul on the road to Damascus). Denny was prayed with and gently fell to the floor for an extended period of time, during which he felt what he described as being infused with intense heat throughout his entire body. The cure was complete, which was puzzling to his doctors and especially to his cancer specialist.

Denny went for many years free of any signs of a break in his remission. However, in early 2017 some pains and concerns brought him back to an oncologist. The prognosis was that the myeloma had returned. This time the drug therapies were much more diverse and able to target specific conditions. The treatments began during the last days of his winter stay in Florida and continued in his home town in Indiana. Through the summer of 2018 there were many prayers and a great deal of support from family and friends. Teresa Rose was at his side throughout the entire time of this end of life trial.

Denny went home to be with the Lord on Oct. 18, 2018. The funeral was held in Indiana, and the eulogy was delivered by his son-in-law. It is added here to illustrate this faithful life. The entire text is published here with the permission and gratitude of the family.

Eulogy for Denny
By Greg

Good Morning. My name is Greg. I am a son-in-law of Denny, and I am humbled by this opportunity to speak on behalf of the family to provide a celebratory summary of Denny.

It is difficult to summarize Denny in just a few words or a few minutes. I am confident that everyone sitting here that was lucky to know Denny could spend hours communicating how Denny affected, impacted or changed their lives. His passion and enthusiasm for life and God were contagious, and he had a way of being able to communicate to all of us.

There are many remarkable things that come to mind, when I think of Denny and the legacy he leaves here on earth:

* A devoted husband who loved Teresa Rose with all his heart. They were always together.
* A father that wanted to provide for his kids and share his love, wisdom, and knowledge on how to be a decent human being and see the good in all.
* A brother that cared for and loved his siblings no matter the ups and downs that a family faces.
* A friend who always had time for you and would help you if you needed anything. And finally….
* His Faith. Without question, Denny wanted to be the best disciple for Jesus Christ that he could be. He loved being a soldier for Jesus Christ.

Denny's faith more than anything is what set him apart. (His commitment, his focus and his passion for his faith).

I distinctly remember the first time I realized that Denny wasn't just quietly going about being a disciple of Christ. I was attending Mass with his daughter before we were married and was sitting next to Denny. When the first song started, I nearly jumped out of my skin when Denny started to belt out the notes. He was so energized and loud. Even all the little kids around Denny would turn and look at Denny with big eyes. No matter, because Denny was in his element and was so enthusiastically participating…just so happy to be in the presence of God.

Like everything, Denny was ALL IN.

Like his business career, ALL IN.

Like his gardening, ALL IN.

Like his healthy diets, ALL IN.

Like his family vacations, ALL IN.

With his faith he was ALL IN. Over time his devotion grew, and he worked hard to be what God wanted him to be. He evangelized to anyone who would listen. He wore a baseball hat that said Jesus is my Boss. His cars had bumper stickers plastered with faith. He wore a large cross around his neck. He wanted everyone to know that he worked for God.

He became a very prayerful man and always had a long list of people he prayed for. I know that list grew and names were changed, but I believe he was praying for 100 or so people.

His commitment for Pro-life that both Denny and Teresa Rose had was remarkable. He loved praying for those struggling women and helping them. It was wonderful to see them both glow when they had an assist in helping a mother change her decision.

He loved Mary and loved praying the rosary. His enthusiasm for this was genuine and pure. Even the last few days when he was not very coherent or could no longer speak, he still could pray the rosary. I witnessed first-hand Denny moving his lips, as we did a rosary with the family. God was present preparing Denny, as Denny was ministering to all of us with devotion to Mary. It was awesome.

Finally, I would like to say that this day is a celebration for Denny. It is hard for all of us to lose a man who was our husband, our father, our brother, and our friend. But Denny wanted nothing more than to be with Jesus. He truly, truly wanted nothing more than to be with Him.

He devoted his life to be a remarkable disciple of God and worked hard, so that he could rise and sit on the lap of Jesus. He set an example that all of us should strive for.

He is looking down on all of us, his hands are in the air, he is smiling ear to ear, shouting,

PRAISE YOU, JESUS! HALLELUJAH!

Thank you all for being here to celebrate Denny.

God Bless You All!

CHAPTER FIVE

Pamela's death under a city bus

I talked with Pamela over lunch at a Catholic conference in Toronto in the spring of 2017. After briefly sharing about my story she also had a dramatic story of her survival from a traffic accident two years earlier.

She had just exited the rear door of a city bus she took daily to her job in downtown Toronto. She slipped on ice and fell to the curb. The driver made his standard right turn and had no idea that anything had happened until horns and lights caught his attention. Pamela had been run over and crushed between the rear tires and the curb. At first there was no sign of life, as she was in shock. Paramedics were on scene soon after the accident. Their first impression was that the victim was dead. Attempts to revive her seemingly lifeless body were successful, but the amount of injury was all too apparent, even to the curious crowd that quickly gathered. The ER room drama was intense, as her vital signs were erratic.

City bus- run- over

Once she had been successfully stabilized and moved to recovery, Pamela was barely coherent as relatives had been notified by looking up the ID information in her purse. She had conveniently included emergency contact names and her parish priest.

After weeks of rehabilitation at the same hospital, Pamela could not walk. She had two broken legs, six broken ribs, and a punctured lung. The healing process was accompanied by many prayers offered by friends and family, including her parish priest. When I met Pamela a few years later, after she had recovered from the trauma and was able to tell that her story had appeared in the local newspapers with the skeptical byline, "this is one to think about." How did Pamela manage to survive being run over by a bus? She and I knew the answer to that rhetorical question and can only praise God for His kindness and mercy.

CHAPTER SIX

Tommy's Near death

We learned about Tommy's story from his widow. We met her after daily Mass at our home north of Toronto. A parked, small station wagon full of personal belongings, and the driver had yet to start her vehicle. The surprise was to find that her license plate was from Mississippi. Her window was open on the chilly morning, so I boldly asked if she was lost. Erin and I were surprised to find that she had spent the night in her car in the church parking lot in order to wait for Mass in the morning. So when we asked if she had already had breakfast, it gave us the opportunity to take her to our local favorite restaurant. The conversation over breakfast revealed that at she had been on the road for weeks all by herself. That night we insisted that she stay in our spare bedroom instead of her car. She had fascinating stories to tell and one was about her deceased husband. It was my blessing to receive the following chapter story to share with you.

Tommy was a field biologist working for the UN on a mission to help out with crop pests in Bolivia in the 1970's. His job was to consult with the land owners whose farms had pest problems. He had been assigned to the wealthy farmers but was also helping the poor and often destitute share croppers from the surrounding farms. On one fateful day Tommy was coaching one of the poor farmers when a well-dressed landowner in a black limo drove onto the scene. Instead of interrupting his conversation he asked the landowner to wait, while he completed his instructions with the poor farmer on how to deal with the pest problems on his small plot. When that was finished, he counseled the man in the limo.

Tommy went back to his hotel where he was told it was not safe to go out in public, because revolutionary soldiers were causing a lot of trouble in the city. He chose to ignore the warning and returned to his temporary UN office in a small courtyard near the local newspaper office. When he arrived he was faced by soldiers with machine guns and told to line up on the wall opposite of his UN office. After a brief prayer in desperation he had a sudden rush of peace and felt transported into the air in some way. It was amazing that he was calm and not panicked in view of the obvious threat that he and the other men in the lineup could be executed at any minute.

The firing squad

This scene of near death for Tommy was halted abruptly by the leader of the revolutionary gunmen in the firing squad lineup. He recognized Tommy from the previous day, as he was the limo driver for the landowner. He had observed that the landowner was made to wait while the poor farmer was instructed on how to save his little crop from destructive bugs.

The driver told the soldiers that Tommy was actually trying to help the common people of Bolivia and not just supporting the oppressive regime of the dictator and his military forces.

Needless to say, Tommy was very relieved that God had answered his prayers. He lived for many more years, as related by his dear wife.

CHAPTER SEVEN

The Near Death of Joe

Accidental death is always very sad and troubling for everyone who is close to the person dying. Joe's near death might have been at the scene of the accident or in an ambulance on the way to a hospital ER.

In his little sedan Joe was calmly crossing a busy intersection on a green light when a transport truck went through a red light and struck Joe's car on the driver's side rear door. The truck was going fast enough to spin the car around several times, leaving it abandoned in the intersection. The car behind his vehicle pushed the still standing car off to the side.

This entire scene was observed by an ambulance crew at a fast-food restaurant across the street. They rushed out the door and put Joe's motionless body into a pressure bag. They were not sure at the time but suspected broken ribs and possible punctured lung. If not treated almost immediately, this injury would surely have caused his death.

Their suspicion was correct, and the solution did save his life. He got to the hospital where the punctured lung was repaired.

After a few days of recuperating, he was discharged and went home.

Joe continues to attend Mass as often as possible and is very thankful that his life was extended for more than the fateful day when he almost became a traffic statistic.

CHAPTER EIGHT

Nick's Sad Lifetime of Near Death

Erin and I were walking in a mall on a rainy day when a lady working in a bakery restaurant noticed my attention to the menu on the wall. She also noticed that I had some difficulty reading the sign, so she handed me the printed version. She commented on the Benedictine crucifix I always wear, which provided an opportunity for telling her that she was talking to a "dead man." That quickly led into her own, personal story of life and death.

This story comes from the fifty-eight year old daughter of a man, who spent a life of dissipation and lived with the effects of constant cigarette smoking, heavy drinking, and unhealthy eating habits for most of his adult life.

Gloria related that she and her mother would make several trips to the hospital each year, following an ambulance in which her dad was yet again a high risk patient. This started when she was only five years old.

This yearly pattern became so common to them that she

could not remember a time when her father was not gasping for breath or in some form of severe pain. The sad irony of his life was that he continued to smoke and drink heavily, paying no attention to his diet nor making any attempts to exercise. Nick was a respiratory and cardiovascular life time disaster. In addition to all of his physical problems, he was constantly angry at just about everything.

Gloria and her mother would pray and go to church, hopeful that prayers might help with this slow-motion family tragedy. The problem was only made worse by the frequent trips to the ER and subsequent attempts to get him to make some effort to improve his destructive life style.

Later when Gloria had a family of her own, she continued to grieve about her mother and father. The tragedy in her life was so great that Gloria had given up on God. With no change for too many years there was little or no hope left. The final stage of her despair was interrupted with a call from a hospital on the day immediately before her father's death.

In a voice that could only be described as a whisper, Nick was able to apologize to Gloria, and ask for her forgiveness for all the pain and suffering he had caused in her life. She could barely speak a consoling word through all of her tears. She did, however, come to some resolution that her dad had finally come to grips with his lifetime of anger and blaming God for all of his problems.

Gloria made it to the hospital ER waiting room, coinciding with the time that her dad's body was being moved to the morgue. Greeted with many tears and hugs from family, she was beginning to be consoled for the life time of regret and resentment surrounding her dad's life time of near death.

She also described an experience her father had recounted of his insight into life after death: that there is another dimension to life when one dies. He shared that during one of the ambulance trips to the hospital, he was separated from his body and floated above the ambulance where he could see himself in his unresponsive, physical body. It was frantically being worked on by paramedics, and he noted that "they were doing it all wrong." Two days later he woke up, discovering that he had returned to his body in a hospital bed.

As Erin and I said good-bye, we were both in tears of joy for Gloria. We continue to marvel at the power of love and the healing strength of forgiveness in relationships between fathers and daughters.

CHAPTER NINE

Death at 82 and Still Living

This account was shared with me at the airport. We were waiting for a flight after the Baptism of our 23rd grandchild in late August 2019. The man sitting next to me was talking on his phone to business partners and the content was easily overheard. He would be back in Ontario in time for the next big sales meeting with the European customers for their product line. After his call ended, I asked him about the type of farm equipment he was selling and installing on site. He was keen to explain his all new and very successful cattle raising program that brought him to Colorado.

He commented about my Benedictine crucifix, which provided an opportunity to use my now well practiced line of evangelism. He seemed open to tell me of his families' faith background. That led to my usually unexpected statement about the person on my end of the conversation: "You are looking at and listening to a dead man." After asking what that meant and hearing my abbreviated story, he seemed quite eager to share his version of end of life in his own family.

When his mother was 82, she was rushed to a hospital with the classic presentation of a heart attack. Their parish priest was the first person called. The pastor arrived to pray with her but she was already dead, and it was too late to hear her last Confession and receive the Last Rite of the Church.

Shortly after the priest left her room, the duty nurse discovered a pulse and additional medical support was rushed to her by the cardiac staff. After a period of stabilization, she was able to have cardiac bypass surgery with complete success.

Her son was happy to report that "she is doing very fine now," fifteen years later. She goes bowling and has many hobbies. He added with a smile and a bit of irony, that after hearing about her car breaking down, he had directed her to the keys for his new Ford Mustang convertible.

His latest project had now become the need for a new car. "Mom has stolen my new Mustang. The first thing I have to do when I get home is to buy another car!"

CHAPTER TEN

Kelly's Near Death and Another on a Horse Cart

P erhaps the most grievous loss of life is when a newborn dies. This tragic story starts with a premature gestation at only seven months with a delivery weight of only two pounds. Kelly had underdeveloped internal organs and lungs that were not prepared for breathing. She was taken out of the delivery room to a trauma unit on another floor.

Her mother was expecting to see her new baby but was told to wait while she was being cleaned up. After what seemed like an eternity she knew something was wrong. A priest had been called and Kelly was given the Last Rites of the Catholic Church even though her mother was Anglican.

With a great deal of medical intervention, Kelly was brought back to life despite the fact that several times during her first hours of life she had to be resuscitated. She was able to leave the hospital after a few weeks of care and monitoring to begin a normal life as a slightly smaller, energetic girl.

The second miraculous event in her life happened when 18

year old Kelly was out riding on her trotting cart in a rural area of Ontario. The horse was spooked by an animal in the thick grass and bolted toward a lake. They collided with a large log on the ground. The horse eventually broke away from the remaining parts of the cart leaving Kelly's badly injured body on the ground with a piece of the metal carriage punctured through her leg. Her first thought was of her mother, and how she would not be able to deal with her only daughter's death.

The horse cart accident

The ability to see from beyond her body was confirmed by being able to observe her mother driving down the road to find help. This would have been impossible from where her battered body lay in the low ditch where the accident happened. Furthermore, she also saw a group of gossamer, human-like figures watching over her and heard a voice say, "You will have pain beyond crying."

Another morning rider had seen the accident and called for medical help. When an ambulance did arrive, Kelly's vital signs were negligible. The paramedics heard the same words coming out of her in a faint voice: "You will have pain beyond crying." During the surreal scene going on before her eyes, she could see herself from above with all the events as clear as if she were actually overhead.

The ER doctors were alarmed at the amount of damage caused by the accident. Part of the metal cart had gone through her leg, and the major damage was the impact with the log, which broke several ribs and punctured several internal organs.

Their conclusion was that they would patch her up and hope for the best. All the time Kelly continued to plead with the consoling figures before her, telling them that she was not ready to leave her life and her dear mother all alone.

After an extended period of recovery, Kelly went on to get married, have a family and continue her life of faith. Her touching witness to me on a chance meeting in response to a car we had for sale in our driveway, led to a series of conversations in which she shared her story of death on a horse cart.

It all started after I showed her the classic car sign I had just improved. When she arrived at the end she was silent for several moments, but then blurted out that she had died too. Following that, she stopped talking.

My next response was to say that her story would be a blessing to include in this book, if she were willing. She did give permission and was given assurance that her real name would not be used to protect her privacy.

As was my experience and has been told by others before, she shared that for many years the emotions involved in her story were so upsetting that she had given up recounting the details to other people. The final straw was a close friend who cut short their friendship after she had shared about this miraculous intervention in her life. Her friends initial response was the clue to her rejection, "that's too spooky for me."

Even as Kelly was telling her story, I could tell she was enthusiastic, but she was also dealing simultaneously with emotions linked to fear. The fear of death remains the ultimate human condition, but Kelly overcame that fear with faith. What else can be said as a reason for the incredible circumstances of her life and death?

Benedictine Crucifix worn daily by the author

Conclusion

The best conclusion is to go back to the opening source quoted from Thomas A Kempis. His work of over four hundred years ago has been for many years my daily devotion and guide for daily inspiration.

Thomas A Kempis

The Imitation of Christ

Translated by Fr. Leo Sherley- Price, Penguin Books, 1952

Book Three, Chapter 30, page 134.

Christ: The mind of man is prone to delusions, but to be deceived by the suggestions of the Devil is a sign of spiritual weakness. Satan does not care whether it be by truth or falsehood that he mocks and deceives you; or whether he obtains your downfall through love of the present or fear of the future. Therefore, let not your heart be troubled, neither let it be afraid. (John xiv,27) Trust in Me and put your whole confidence in My mercy. (Ps.xci,2) When you think I am far away, then often I am nearest to you. And when you think the battle almost lost when anything turns out contrary to your plans. Therefore do not allow your feelings of the moment to obscure your judgment, nor yield to depression as though all hope of recovery were lost.

After all that has been told of life and death with faith in Jesus Christ, the best conclusion is that

No matter what happens,

Immanuel (God is with us).

"Create in me a clean heart, O God,

and put a new and right spirit within me" (Psalm 51:10).

"Let the words of my mouth,

and the meditation of my heart be acceptable in Thy sight,

O Lord, my rock and my Redeemer" (Psalm 19:14)

THE END

Or is it?

You can email Dr. John Haart and he will get back to you: drjohnhaart@gmail.com.

Printed in the United States
By Bookmasters